MY BODY, MY RULES

I MAKE GOOD CHOICES

BY
LAYLA
OWENS

Enslow
PUBLISHING

Please visit our website, www.enslow.com.
For a free color catalog of all our high-quality books, call toll free 1-800-398-2504 or fax 1-877-980-4454.

Library of Congress Cataloging-in-Publication Data

Names: Owens, Layla, author.
Title: I make good choices / Layla Owens.
Description: Buffalo, NY : Enslow Publishing, [2026] | Series: My body, my rules | Includes index. | Audience term: Children
Identifiers: LCCN 2024053436 (print) | LCCN 2024053437 (ebook) | ISBN 9781978543836 (library binding) | ISBN 9781978543829 (paperback) | ISBN 9781978543843 (ebook)
Subjects: LCSH: Decision making–Juvenile literature. | Critical thinking in children–Juvenile literature. | Problem solving in children–Juvenile literature.
Classification: LCC BF448 .O96 2026 (print) | LCC BF448 (ebook) | DDC 153.8/3–dc23/eng/20241231
LC record available at https://lccn.loc.gov/2024053436
LC ebook record available at https://lccn.loc.gov/2024053437

Published in 2026 by
Enslow Publishing
2544 Clinton Street
Buffalo, NY 14224

Designer: Tanya Dellaccio Keeney
Editor: Caitie McAneney

Photo credits: Series art (notebook) Design PRESENT/Shutterstock.com; series art (stickers) tmn art/Shutterstock.com; cover Luis Molinero/Shutterstock.com; p. 5 Sorapop Udomsri/Shutterstock.com; p. 7 FamVeld/Shutterstock.com; p. 9 kornnphoto/Shutterstock.com; p. 11 Piotr Wawrzyniuk/Shutterstock.com; p. 13 PeopleImages.com - Yuri A/Shutterstock.com; p. 15 Krakenimages.com/Shutterstock.com; p. 17 mike mols/Shutterstock.com; p. 19 polkadot_photo/Shutterstock.com; p. 21 Sklo Studio/Shutterstock.com.

Printed in the United States of America

CPSIA compliance information: Batch #CSENS26: For further information contact Enslow Publishing, at 1-800-398-2504.

CONTENTS

I CAN CHOOSE 4
ASK QUESTIONS 6
IS IT SAFE? 8
MIA STAYS SAFE 10
PROS AND CONS 12
TREY TRUSTS HIS GUT 14
OUTCOMES 16
TESS TALKS IT OUT 18
FEEL CONFIDENT! 20
WORDS TO KNOW 22
FOR MORE INFORMATION 23
INDEX 24

BOLDFACE WORDS APPEAR IN WORDS TO KNOW.

I CAN CHOOSE

As you grow up, you will need to make more choices. What sport do you want to play? Who will you be friends with? Some choices are easy. Others are much harder. You can practice making good choices every day.

MAKING GOOD CHOICES TAKES **CRITICAL THINKING**. THIS IS AN IMPORTANT LIFE SKILL!

ASK QUESTIONS

Think about an easy choice. Should you wear a coat? Ask yourself questions: What do I have to do today? Is it warm or cold? If you will be outside in the cold, wearing a coat is a good choice.

ASK YOURSELF: WHAT WILL MAKE MY BODY FEEL GOOD AND COMFORTABLE?

IS IT SAFE?

Safety is the most important thing to think about when you make a choice. Think about safety rules. Don't go with strangers. Always tell your parents where you are going. Don't do things that might hurt yourself or others.

YOU MIGHT NOT WANT TO WEAR A HELMET, BUT IT IS A GOOD CHOICE. IT KEEPS YOU SAFE.

MIA STAYS SAFE

Mia walks to school each day. She can run ahead alone. Then she can see her friends sooner. Or, she can wait for her big sister. Mia asks herself: Which choice is safer? She waits for her sister. They walk together.

MIA KNOWS SHE MADE A GOOD CHOICE. SHE FEELS SAFE WITH HER SISTER.

PROS AND CONS

Think about all the good things that could happen if you do something. Those are "pros." Think of all the things that might happen that aren't so good. Those are "cons." Make a list of pros and cons to help you decide.

IMAGINE YOU WANT TO JOIN A SOCCER TEAM. THE "PROS" ARE PLAYING SOCCER AND MAKING NEW FRIENDS. THE "CON" IS BEING BUSY AFTER SCHOOL.

TREY TRUSTS HIS GUT

Sometimes your "gut" will help you make a good choice. Trey's friends tell him to pull a **prank** on a teacher. It sounds funny at first. But Trey feels uncomfortable. His gut says it is not the right thing to do.

FOLLOWING YOUR "GUT" MEANS LISTENING TO YOUR INNER VOICE. IT CAN TELL YOU IF SOMETHING FEELS RIGHT OR WRONG.

OUTCOMES

Imagine the **outcomes** of each choice. Good choices have positive, or good, outcomes for you and for others around you. Ask yourself: What might happen to me? What might happen to others? Will it help or hurt?

IMAGINE YOU SKIP YOUR HOMEWORK TO PLAY VIDEO GAMES. WHAT MIGHT THE OUTCOME BE?

TESS TALKS IT OUT

You can talk about your choice with a friend or trusted adult. Tess sees her sister doing something **dangerous**. Should she tell her parents? She asks her friend Jay. He says letting her parents know will keep her sister safe. Tess agrees.

TEACHERS AND PARENTS CAN GIVE GOOD **ADVICE.**

FEEL CONFIDENT!

Practice making small choices. What will you wear? What will you eat? Then, you can feel **confident** in your ability to make bigger choices. If you make a mistake, that's okay! You can learn from it.

PRACTICE LISTENING TO YOUR GUT. IT CAN HELP YOU WHEN YOU HAVE A BIG CHOICE TO MAKE!

WORDS TO KNOW

advice: An idea or opinion that someone gives to help you decide what to do.

confident: Believing one can succeed.

critical thinking: The act or practice of applying reason to deal with a problem or information.

dangerous: Unsafe.

outcome: Something that follows as a result of something else.

prank: A trick or joke done for fun.

FOR MORE INFORMATION

BOOKS

Emminizer, Theresa. *I Trust My Feelings*. Buffalo, NY: Enslow Publishing, 2025.

Ridley, Sarah. *Being Safe.* New York: NY: PowerKids Press, 2023.

WEBSITES

How to Make Better Decisions
www.youtube.com/watch?v=XSQbQ78GFLg
Watch this video to learn more about responsible decision-making.

Talking About Your Feelings
kidshealth.org/en/kids/talk-feelings.html
Identifying and talking about feelings can help you make good choices. Learn more about how to talk about feelings with this website!

Publisher's note to educators and parents: Our editors have carefully reviewed these websites to ensure that they are suitable for students. Many websites change frequently, however, and we cannot guarantee that a site's future contents will continue to meet our high standards of quality and educational value. Be advised that students should be closely supervised whenever they access the internet.

INDEX

advice, 19
confidence, 20
critical thinking, 5
helmets, 9
friends, 4, 10, 13, 18
gut, 14, 15, 21
inner voice, 15
mistakes, 20
outcomes, 16
parents, 18, 19
prank, 14
pros and cons, 12, 13
questions, 6
safety, 8, 9, 10, 11, 18
soccer, 13
sports, 4
strangers, 8
teachers, 14, 19